MW00472970

Conversation Starters

for

Atul Gawande's

Being Mortal

By dailyBooks

  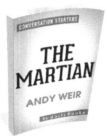

Every purchase comes with a FREE download of the hottest titles!

Add spice to any conversation
Never run out of things to say
Spend time with those you love

Read it for FREE on any smartphone, tablet, Kindle, PC or Mac.
No purchase necessary - licensed for personal enjoyment only.

Tips for Using dailyBooks Conversation Starters:

EVERY GOOD BOOK CONTAINS A WORLD FAR DEEPER THAN the surface of its pages. The characters and their world come alive through the words on the pages, yet the characters and its world still live on. Questions herein are designed to bring us beneath the surface of the page and invite us into the world that lives on. These questions can be used to:

- Foster a deeper understanding of the book
- Promote an atmosphere of discussion for groups
- Assist in the study of the book, either individually or corporately
- Explore unseen realms of the book as never seen before

About Us:

THROUGH YEARS OF EXPERIENCE AND FIELD EXPERTISE, from newspaper featured book clubs to local library chapters, *dailyBooks* can bring your book discussion to life. Host your book party as we discuss some of today's most widely read books.

Table of Contents

Introducing *Being Mortal*

IN *BEING MORTAL*, ATUL GAWANDE DISCUSSES THE transformation of medicine in modern times that helps people live better lives but also urges for the improvement of medicine for lives when they are at their end. Gawande says that medicine has improved greatly in the modern world. There are more births, injuries are healed better and faster, serious illnesses and diseases can be managed or cured; however, the care for aging people needs huge improvements.

Atul Gawande talks about nursing homes where patients have been forced to live in their beds or wheelchairs because the homes are concerned about safety. A negative aspect of some hospitals is the isolation of dying people. They often only check vital signs after the possibility of a cure has been long gone. There are also doctors who are so adamant about healing or curing patients that they perform procedures that only prolong suffering.

In Gawande's opinion, the quality of a human life should be placed above everything else. He says this is the ultimate limitation of medical practitioners. Gawande offers solutions that will give the elderly and physically disabled more freedom and a greater quality of life. He discusses hospice care as well and shows that a person can live a "rich and dignified life" in their last days. Gawande believes that a person at any age has more importance in life than being safe and staying alive for a longer length of time.

In Gawande's view of life, human lives are meaningful because of the moments they have. If a person were to focus on the small minute-by-minute measure of pleasure or pain, they would miss the story or purpose in a person's life. Gawande believes that each person plays a meaningful role, and each life has a purpose. Gawande also believes that a person should have control over what happens in their life even though they may not have control over every circumstance in life.

In Gawande's words, Being Mortal is about the struggle to accept the inevitable death humans face. Gawande acknowledges that scientific advancements in medicine have allowed people to push against the human body's limitations, which was part of why he became a doctor. However, he recognizes the failure of medical professionals to realize those limitations will always exist, as well as the damage that they can do. Medical professionals have been wrong in believing that their job was to ensure the safety and health of the population. Instead, Gawande's opinion is that medical professionals must ensure the well-being of the population.

Introducing the Author

IN BROOKLYN, NEW YORK, IN 1965, ATUL GAWANDE WAS born to Indian immigrants. His parents were both doctors. Even though Gawande was born in New York, his family spent most of his childhood in Athens, Ohio. He graduated from the local high school in 1983. He then went on to Stanford University, where he graduated in 1987 with a degree in Biology and Political Science. He studied at the University of Oxford in England as a Rhodes Scholar. He obtained a master's in economics, philosophy, and politics in 1989. From there, he went on to study at Harvard University where he became a Doctor of Medicine in 1995. In 1999, he earned his master's in public health, and eventually, became a surgeon.

During his undergraduate studies, Atul Gawande worked for numerous political figures on their campaigns including Gary Hart, Al Gore, and Bill Clinton. He was Bill Clinton's healthcare lieutenant. He then began working at the Department of Health and Human Services as their senior advisor. He currently works at the World Health Organization as a director for the Global Patient Safety Challenge department.

Atul Gawande began working at *The New Yorker* as a staff writer and journalist in 1998. This opportunity came after an article he wrote was published in *Slate*. In one essay for *The New Yorker*, he compared the healthcare in two Texas locations. The article caught the attention of United States President, Barack Obama, who cited it in his speech for healthcare reform. Gawande has also been published in the *New England Journal of Medicine* for military surgery techniques, error in medicine, and many more topics.

In 2002, Atul Gawande's first book, *A Surgeon's Notes on an Imperfect Science*, was published. It became a finalist for the National Book Award. In 2007, his second book, *Better* was published and in 2009, *The Checklist Manifesto* was published. This was Gawande's third book. It became a bestseller for *The New York Times* in 2010. In 2014, Gawande's most recent book release, *Being Mortal: Medicine and What Matters in the End* was published.

Discussion Questions

. . . .

question 1

Atul Gawande believes that at the end of a person's life, doctors should
ensure well-being and not just health and safety. What do you think the role
of a doctor is when one nears the end of their life?

. . . .

. . . .

question 2

Atul Gawande discusses the medical field at length in *Being Mortal*. What did you learn from reading this book? What did you find most interesting?

. . . .

. . . .

question 3

In *Being Mortal*, Atul Gawande defines courage as being strong even though
there are many things to be afraid of. He defines wisdom as careful strength.
How would you define courage? How would you define wisdom?

. . . .

question 4

In *Being Mortal*, Atul Gawande says that life is made up of continuous choices that must be made. Do you agree? Why or why not?

question 5

In *Being Mortal*, Atul Gawande states that the focus of medicine is to fight against diseases, and ultimately, death. Medical professionals view death as an enemy but forget that death will always win eventually. Gawande says it is better to be someone who recognizes when to surrender than to continue to fight when fighting will do more damage. What are your thoughts on these quotations?

question 6

Atul Gawande says that life is meaningful for people because of the story it
tells through moments. If one were to measure each moment by how happy
or sad they were in each second, it would be less meaningful. What are your
thoughts on this statement?

question 7

Do you feel as though Atul Gawande's ideas in *Being Mortal* are controversial in any way? If so, which side of the controversy do you agree with?

question 8

Atul Gawande proposes many solutions to the problems that occur in the medical field during the end of one's life. Do you think it is possible for these solutions to be implemented? Do you feel they would be successful?

question 9

Atul Gawande addresses many concerns about end-of-life care in *Being Mortal*. What do you think about his concerns? Which of his concerns do you find the most pressing?

question 10

Atul Gawande presents statistics that state that 25% of Medicare spending goes towards 5% of patients at the end of his or her life. What are your thoughts on these statistics?

· ·

question 11

Atul Gawande presents the issues and limitations that doctors face in the
modern world. Did your opinion of doctors change in any way after reading
this book?

· ·

. . . .

question 12

Being Mortal discusses the end of life and how it should be handled. Has
your view on how you would like your final stages of your own life to be
changed? If so, what changed?

. . . .

question 13

In the final scene of *Being Mortal*, Atul Gawande tells the story of his father and how he fulfilled his father's wishes. What are your thoughts on this story?

question 14

In *Being Mortal*, Atul Gawande states that the medical field has "medicalized mortality." What do you think is meant by this statement?

question 15

Gawande states in *Being Mortal* that he learned about many things relating to the medical field, but he never learned about "being mortal." What are your thoughts on this statement? Should medical schools include end-of-life care in their curriculum?

question 16

Some readers recommended this book for adults of all ages, not just those who are older, elderly, or taking care of those at the end of life. What are your thoughts on who could enjoy this book?

question 17

One reader commented that Atul Gawande handled a grim topic with grace. What do you think of Gawande's way of handling the topic of mortality?

question 18

One reader wished Atul Gawande would be more "scathing" in his critiques of bad experiences he has witnessed in end-of-life care. What are your thoughts on this?

question 19

One reader said that *Being Mortal* is the most important book on mortality to date. Do you agree with this statement?

question 20

One reader called *Being Mortal* a "must read." Do you agree with this statement? Why do you think this information should be read by everyone?

 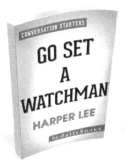 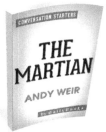

. . . .

question 21

One reader made the comment that she was apprehensive about reading a book that tackled the depressing topic of mortality. Did you feel any apprehension or discomfort about mortality prior to or while reading *Being Mortal*?

. . . .

question 22

Many readers have called *Being Mortal* "eye opening." Do you agree with this statement? If so, in what ways did it open your eyes to the issues presented?

question 23

Many readers enjoyed the real-life stories of people facing end-of-life care. What did you think of these stories?

. . . .

question 24

One reader did not like the inclusion of the history of assisted living. What were your thoughts on the discussion of the history of assisted living in *Being Mortal?*

. . . .

question 25

One reader wanted more to be written on the psychological aspect of aging and the fear of dying. What are your thoughts on this?

question 26

Atul Gawande became a Rhodes Scholar and studied at Stanford and Harvard. Do you think his education at prestigious institutes gave him a greater chance at success?

question 27

Atul Gawande worked for many political figures during his undergraduate studies. What do you think of his work with political figures? How do you think these experiences helped shape his opinions?

question 28

Atul Gawande started writing for *The New Yorker* in 1998. His article on healthcare captured the attention of President Barack Obama. What are your thoughts on this? Do you think this helped his career?

question 29

Atul Gawande was the senior adviser at the Department of Health and Human Services and is currently the director of the World Health Organization Global Patient Safety Challenge. How do you think these positions helped his career?

question 30

Atul Gawande studied biology, political science, philosophy, economics, and medicine. What are your thoughts on his education choices?

question 31

Atul Gawande shared the story of Susan Block's father in *Being Mortal*. He stated that he would endure many difficult circumstances with his health provided he was still able to do the things he enjoyed. Would you continue to live if you could still do the activities you loved? When would it be enough for you?

question 32

In *Being Mortal*, Atul Gawande says that it is difficult for doctors to know when to surrender because they are always fighting against death. If you were in the same position as these doctors, how would you make this decision?

question 33

In *Being Mortal*, Atul Gawande discusses how to ensure that the elderly and disabled have a better quality of life and how to consider their well-being in the final stages of life. If you were in the position to care for someone who is in their final stages, or if you already have been in that position, what decisions would you make to ensure well-being?

question 34

Atul Gawande discusses mortality. How do you view aging? How does your view of aging differ as you get older?

question 35

An anecdotal story in *Being Mortal* is the story of Felix and Bella. Felix had to retire to care for his ailing wife, Bella. In your life, have you known stories similar to Felix and Bella? How do you think you would handle the situation if you were Felix?

question 36

In *Being Mortal*, Atul Gawande presents the story of Alice Hobson, who was independent until her late 70s. One day, she fell and lost her independence. Her family gave her the option to live in a facility or live with them. If you were Alice, what would you choose?

question 37

In *Being Mortal*, Atul Gawande presents the story of Keren Wilson and her assisted living facility designed with her aging mother in mind. If you were in need of an assisted living facility, how would you feel about living at Keren Wilson's facility?

question 38

When Atul Gawande discusses Sara Monopoli's end-of-life care, he asks what Sarah and her doctors should do next. What would you choose to do with Sara's care?

Quiz Questions

. . . .

question 39

In *Being Mortal*, Atul Gawande discusses the transformation of
_____ in today's world that helps people live better lives.
Gawande also wants care for lives when they are at their end to be improved.

. . . .

question 40

True or False: Atul Gawande discusses nursing homes where patients have been forced to live in their beds or wheelchairs because the homes are solely concerned about safety.

question 41

True or False: Atul Gawande believes that the focus should be on keeping patients alive for as long as possible when they are the end of their lives.

question 42

True or False: Atul Gawande believes that a person's life is more than how long they can be kept alive.

question 43

True or False: Atul Gawande believes that a person's life is made up of
significant moments.

question 44

True or False: In Atul Gawande's opinion, it should be up to the doctors how long a person should stay alive. They should have total control over a person's health.

question 45

True or False: Atul Gawande recognizes that doctors often have a failure to recognize that there will always be limits to what they can do for a person.

question 46

The author of *Being Mortal* is _____. He was born
in Brooklyn, New York, in 1965.

question 47

The author studied _____ and political science at Stanford University. He studied _____ at Harvard University.

question 48

Atul Gawande worked on the campaigns of Gary Hart, Al Gore, and
_____. He then became the senior adviser for the
Department of Health and Human Services under the Clinton presidency.

question 49

True or False: Atul Gawande wrote an article on healthcare for *The New Yorker*.

question 50

True or False: Atul Gawande published his first book, *Being Mortal,* in 2014.

Quiz Answers

1. Medicine
2. True
3. False; Atul Gawande believes the focus should be on well-being for end-of-life patients.
4. True
5. True
6. False; Atul Gawande believes that people should have control over their lives even when they cannot control every circumstance in life.
7. True
8. Atul Gawande
9. biology; medicine
10. Bill Clinton
11. True
12. False; *Being Mortal* is Gawande's fourth book.

THE END

Want to promote your book group? Register here.

PLEASE LEAVE US A FEEDBACK.

THANK YOU!

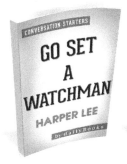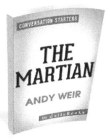

Made in the USA
Las Vegas, NV
17 February 2023

67671203R00039